Finance

for

Non Financial
Public Sector
Managers

Finance

for

Non Financial
Public Sector
Managers

Essential skills for the public sector

Jennifer Bean
Lascelles Hussey

PUBLICATIONS

HB PUBLICATIONS
(Incorporated as Givegood Limited)

Published by

**HB Publications
London, England**

British Library Cataloguing in Publication Data

ISBN 1 899448 03 9

Printed and bound in England by Antony Rowe Ltd.

Contents

Chapter 1

INTRODUCTION

Finance is a vital resource for every organisation and it is therefore important that all staff, particularly managers, should have an understanding of finance. Often finance remains the domain of a few, and non-financial managers are not normally involved in financial issues. This book is therefore designed to assist non-financial managers to gain a basic understanding of key financial concepts that affect an organisation's day to day operations.

The public sector has undergone many changes in recent years with respect to commercialisation and accountability. These changes have included increased competition with market testing and compulsory competitive tendering; the creation of Health Service Trusts and GP Fund Holders; and an increase in public services being delivered by the private sector to name a few. It is becoming increasingly important for all public sector organisations to demonstrate that they are financially viable entities in their own right. This means that income, regardless of its source, can fully support all expenditure, and that value for money services can be provided to meet the requirements of end users.

Managers from a non-financial background need to have a financial awareness to ensure that the financial implications of service decisions are taken into account. This book covers the most important aspects of financial accounting. In the final chapter, key financial terms and expressions are demystified in order to help managers communicate with finance professionals.

In addition to providing a practical text with illustrations, the book also incorporates exercises at the end of each chapter to enable the manager to practice some of the techniques covered and apply the concepts to his/her work situation. Where appropriate suggested solutions are given at the end of the book.

Chapter 2

KEEPING THE ACCOUNTS

Keeping Financial Records

Organisations tend to maintain on an on-going basis financial records which keep account of all their transactions. It is these financial records which are used to develop the key financial statements for the organisation. The two main financial statements produced by all public sector organisations are the income and expenditure account (similar to a profit and loss account for a private sector organisation) and the balance sheet. The income and expenditure account is a statement showing the surplus or deficit arising as a result of the organisation's activities over a period of time, for example a year. The balance sheet, on the other hand, gives a statement of assets and liabilities at a particular point in time, for example, the last day of the financial year. Both these statements are discussed in more detail in chapters 3 and 4 respectively.

Maintaining proper financial records are essential for the following reasons:

❖ They provide the basis for the management accounts which are produced on a regular basis, monthly, quarterly, etc.

❖ They form the basis for the financial statements that have to be produced at least once per year

❖ They provide a record of what has actually occurred within the organisation in financial terms

❖ They are essential to ensuring accountability and protection against fraud

❖ They provide the information required for financial monitoring and control

❖ They provide an audit trail for each financial transaction that takes place

Financial Transactions

Most large organisations now operate computerised financial recording systems, however, many small organisations may still maintain manual systems. All financial recording systems whether computerised or manual are based on basic double entry book-keeping principles.

Double entry refers to the fact that each transaction requires two entries in the accounting system.

Book-keeping refers to the maintenance of accounting records which historically were kept in books or ledgers.

This book will not attempt to cover the theory of double entry book-keeping, however, we illustrate the process for recording transactions using double entry principles with the following example.

A school has set up a charity account to supplement it's income for which separate records are being kept. Each transaction that has taken place is recorded in a red book such that a set of charity accounts can be produced at the end of the year. The first month's transactions and the accounting entries that were made are given as follows:

Month 1	Transactions	Accounting Implications	
4th	Donations were received of £500	Income increases by £500	Cash increases by £500
9th	Models and toys were sold for £250	Income increases by £250	Cash increases by £250
10th	Prize for a raffle was purchased for £100	Expenditure on prizes £100	Cash decreases by £100
14th	Raffle tickets were sold raising £500	Income increases by £500	Cash increases by £500
20th	An invoice of £50 was paid for the hire of stalls	Expenditure on hire charges £50	Cash decreases by £50
27th	A new globe was purchased for the geography classroom for £100	Expenditure on equipment £100	Cash decreases by £100
28th	A new video was purchased for the media classroom for £300	Expenditure on equipment £300	Cash decreases by £300

At the end of the month it is possible to calculate the following:
- Total income for the month is £1,250 (£500 + £250 + £500)
- There has been expenditure on a range of items. (Depending on the organisation, some of the expenditure would be regarded as capital expenditure whilst others would be classified as revenue expenditure)

- In this example, total expenditure is £550 (£100 + £50 + £100 + £300)

The Financial Statements

As previously mentioned, the two key financial statements are the income and expenditure account and the balance sheet. These statements have to be produced at least once a year, and most organisations are required to have the statements audited by an independent auditor to ensure that they give a "true and fair" view of the organisation's activities for the period concerned.

The format of the financial statements will vary from one organisation to another, however, standard terms and layouts which comply with accounting standards are commonly used. An example format for the two statements is shown as follows:

Income and Expenditure Account

	£	£	
INCOME			
Sales		1,000	
Less: Cost of Sales		400	
Gross Profit		600	
Grants		8,000	
Fees and Charges		4,000	
Interest		400	
Rent		-	
Total Income		13,000	**A**
EXPENDITURE			
Employee Costs	5,500		
Transport Costs	500		
Accommodation Costs	2,000		
Goods and Services	3,000		
Central & Support Service Costs	400		
Sundry Expenses	800		
Finance Charges	200		
Depreciation	300		
Bad Debts	100		
Total Expenditure		12,800	**B**
Surplus for the Year		200	**A-B**

Balance Sheet Format

	£	£	£	
Fixed Assets *				
Land and Buildings			4,250	
Plant and Machinery			400	
Motor Vehicles			1,300	
Equipment, Fixtures and Fittings			800	
Total Fixed Assets			6,750	
Current Assets				
Stock	0			
Debtors	3,000			
Cash	50			
		3,050		
Current Liabilities				
Creditors	2,000			
Overdraft	800			
		2,800		
Net Current Assets			250	
Total Net Assets			7,000	A
Represented by:				
Reserves b/f		1,800		
Surplus for the year		200		
Accumulated reserves c/f			2,000	
Specific Funds			1,000	
Long Term Loans			4,000	
			7,000	B

A always equals B

* Fixed Assets are stated after depreciation has been deducted from the cost

The exact format of the income and expenditure account may differ from organisation to organisation and also the statements may be given different names. For example, a local authority income and expenditure account is usually referred to as a "revenue account".

SUMMARY

❒ The two main financial statements produced by all public sector organisations are the income and expenditure account and the balance sheet

❒ The income and expenditure account is a statement showing the surplus or deficit arising as a result of the organisation's activities over a period of time

❒ The balance sheet gives a statement of assets and liabilities at a particular point in time

❒ All financial recording systems whether computerised or manual are based on basic double entry book-keeping

Exercise 1

Accounting Entries

For the following scenarios identify the accounting entries, i.e. identify which accounts will be affected.

For example, if a housing manager pays a builder £1,000 to undertake repairs, the accounting entries will be

Increase in repairs expenditure account	*£1,000*
Decrease in asset of cash	*£1,000*

a)   A fire officer purchases new uniforms for £10,000 but has yet to pay the supplier.

b)   A doctor charges £50 for writing a letter on behalf of a client for which the client had to pay in advance.

c)   A school contracts out its cleaning services to a private contractor and has to pay £24,000 a year in monthly instalments. Show the entries for this month.

d)   The planning department advised three clients during the week all of whom were charged £200 each. Two paid immediately however, the third has yet to pay.

e)   Three managers of the local authority grounds maintenance service decide to set up their own company in order to bid independently for contracts. To start it off, they all invest £10,000 each in the new company.

Suggested solutions to this exercise can be found on page 123

Exercise 2

Financial Records

In order to gain an understanding of financial accounting within your organisation, undertake the following activities:

⏵ Describe the type of financial accounting systems which exist in your organisation

⏵ Is the system based on cash accounting principles?　　　Yes ☐　　No ☐

(This means that throughout the year the system only accounts for cash transactions; that is it does not take account of debtors and creditors, only those orders which have been paid for or income actually received)

➠ Does the system operate accruals accounting?　　　　　Yes ❑　No ❑

(This means that income and expenditure are accounted for as they arise and not as they are paid for, i.e. debtors and creditors are established throughout the year)

➠ Are there commitment accounting facilities?　　　　　Yes ❑　No ❑

(Does the system take account of orders yet to be paid for)

➠ Obtain a copy of the organisations financial statements and read them ensuring that you understand all the statements and the headings used.

Exercise 3

Which Financial Statement?

For each of the following items, identify which of the financial statements they belong to - the Income and Expenditure account (I&E) or the Balance Sheet (B/S); simply tick the appropriate boxes.

	Income and Expenditure	Balance Sheet
Cash in bank		
Fees		
Motor vehicles		
Creditors		
Stationery		
Rent		
Grants		
Overdraft		
Computer maintenance		
Depreciation		
Debtors		
Office furniture		
Insurance		
Loan		
Bank interest		
Salaries		
Reserves		

Suggested solutions to this exercise can be found on page 125

Chapter 3

THE INCOME AND EXPENDITURE ACCOUNT

The income and expenditure account reflects all the income "earned" by the organisation in a particular period, for example, one year. Income includes monies from all the activities and trades including any other income that may be earned such as interest earned on deposit accounts, investment income derived from investments, and rents earned from property. It also reflects all the expenditure incurred in pursuance of those trades and other activities.

The difference between the income and expenditure is either a surplus or a deficit defined as follows:

Surplus ⇨ *Where income exceeds expenditure*

Deficit ⇨ *Where expenditure exceeds income*

Elements of an Income and Expenditure Account

The two simple definitions to remember in respect of income and expenditure are as follows.

Income	⇨	**what is earned by the organisation**
Expenditure	⇨	**what is used by the organisation**

The income earned in respect of the trades and activities and the expenditure used up in order to undertake the trades and activities should be calculated over the same time period. This principle is called the "matching concept". Hence, all income for the year ending 31 March 1997 is matched against the expenditure for the same period in order to arrive at the surplus or deficit for the year.

Public sector organisations can derive income from a wide range of sources. Many public sector organisations are publicly funded and therefore receive government grants or subsidies, others have to be self sufficient and gain their income directly from the trade or activity which they are involved in. This means charging for services by contracting with other bodies or gaining revenues directly from the user.

Income tends to fall into the following main categories:

Grants

Grants are given by Central Government, Local Government and other grant giving bodies such as the Lottery Board. The level of grant received may vary each year depending on many external factors outside the organisation's control. Where the organisation is dependent on grant income they are subject to the policies and strategies of the grant giver.

Fees and charges

Fees and charges may be levied for the use of services rendered. These could relate to one-off projects or may be the basis for a large proportion of the organisation's income, in which case a charging policy will be required.

Sales

This term tends to relate to the income derived from the sale of products as opposed to services.

Interest

Interest will arise from straight forward bank and building society deposits, money market deposits, etc.

Rents

If the organisation has property which is used by a third party it is normal to charge a rent for such use. In addition to rents there may also be service charges if the property benefits from services such as heating and lighting of common parts.

Dividends

Where an organisation holds investments it will usually receive investment income. In the case of shares, this income is called a dividend.

The total income earned in respect of the organisation's principal activity is sometimes referred to as "turnover", with the other income being referred to as "other income".

When constructing an income and expenditure account, it should be noted that the income for a particular period relates to everything that has been earned in the period and does not necessarily equal the cash received. Quite often, monies due from a variety of sources such as customers and grant funders may be outstanding at any one moment in time; monies due and not yet received are referred to as **debtors**. This is illustrated by the following example.

A doctors practice has a contract with the local health authority for which a formula grant is given based on the number of NHS patients registered. The practice also provides a range of other therapeutic services such as osteopathy and counselling for which patients have to pay. Income is also generated from the Doctor's private patients. The grants due for the year are £240,000 paid in four instalments of £60,000 per quarter, the final quarter is always received in the month after the year end. All other fees and charges are paid on demand but from time to time some credit arrangements are made whereby patients are given up to three months to pay their bills. During this year the total bills raised by the practice totalled £240,000 of which £60,000 remained unpaid at the end of the year.

The actual income for the practice for the year is, therefore, £480,000, however the cash received is only £360,000 as £60,000 of the grant and £60,000 of bills has not been received by the end of the year.

In the same way as income for a year relates to what is earned as opposed to the cash received by the organisation, expenditure relates to what is used as opposed to the cash spent by the organisation. It is quite common for organisations not to pay their suppliers immediately even though the goods have been received or services used; monies due to suppliers etc. are referred to as **creditors**.

This type of day to day expenditure which is used up by the organisation as it delivers services is called revenue expenditure. This is distinct from capital expenditure which relates to the purchase of assets. The main categories of revenue expenditure can be summarised under these headings:

Employee Costs
Including all expenses relating to employees including salaries, national insurance, pension contributions, car allowances etc.

Transport Costs
Including all expenses relating to transport such as car leases, hire charges, etc.

Supplies and Services
Includes expenditure on consumable items used in the delivery of the service, and other services such as marketing, advertising and so on.

Accommodation Costs
Includes all costs relating to the accommodation such as rent, rates, utilities, etc.

Support Service Costs
Depending on the nature of the organisation there may be separate supporting services. These services include personnel, finance, legal, and so on.

Financing Costs
These costs relate to the cost of any borrowings made by the organisation such as interest charges, bank charges and so on.

Other Costs
There are many general costs which may not fit into the above categories such as subscriptions, sundries, etc.

There are generally two types of basis for recording transactions, one is cash accounting and the other accruals accounting. They differ in the following ways:

Cash Accounting
Transactions are recorded when they have been paid or received, i.e. when the cash transaction has taken place. This system does not take account of debtors and creditors throughout the year. However, at the end of the year a one-off adjustment is made with respect to outstanding debtors and creditors at that point in time.

Accruals Accounting
Transactions are recorded as they occur as opposed to when they have been paid for or received. This requires the identification of accounts payable (creditors) and accounts receivable (debtors). By operating accruals accounting, the full extent of income and expenditure can be established throughout the year.

Preparing the Income and Expenditure Account

The income and expenditure account may be prepared at any time and for any period, however, it is usual that it is produced at least annually.

In order to produce the income and expenditure account, the organisation's books of account will be "closed off" for the period or periods to which the income and expenditure account relates. To ensure that all the relevant income and expenditure for the period is correctly reflected in the income and expenditure account adjustments may be made to some of the accounts. The types of accounting adjustments that are regularly made are summarised as follows:

Accruals

An accrual has the effect of increasing the level of expenditure for items that have been used but have yet to be invoiced by the supplier. An example of this is the telephone charge. If the telephone bill is not made up to the end of the accounting period then there will be some usage that has not been billed and this is accrued for.

Debtors

Adjustments are made to income to reflect monies due but not yet received. This has the impact of increasing income.

Creditors

Adjustments are made for monies owing to third parties but not yet paid. This has the effect of increasing expenditure.

Prepayments

Like accruals, when monies have been paid in advance, then an adjustment needs to be made to reflect the advance portion. For example, at the end of March a telephone bill is paid which includes the line rental costs for March to June. This represents an advance payment or prepayment and the telephone expenditure needs to be reduced by the amount of the prepayment.

Depreciation

Where an organisation has fixed assets such as cars, furniture and fittings etc. the value of these assets need to be reduced to reflect the wear and tear they encounter during normal usage. This is referred to as depreciation and is shown as an expenditure item.

Bad Debts

An organisation may have customers who fail to pay outstanding monies. The organisation may then be forced to create a provision for bad debts to reflect the possibility of non payment or to write off specific bad debts from customers who fail to pay.

Key Uses of the Income and Expenditure Account

All organisations are required to produce financial statements each year and therefore they will always produce an income and expenditure account at least once a year. The key uses of this statement are as follows:

❖ It sets out the surplus or deficit made during the year

❖ It shows the key sources of income earned by the organisation

❖ It identifies the key areas of expenditure

❖   When compared with previous years it identifies areas of growth and reduction in both income sources and expenditure areas

❖   If targets are set in respect of income and expenditure levels, it can be used as a performance measure

The Trading Account

The trading account can be defined as an account of one's trade. An account in financial terms refers to a record, and a trade refers to the principal activity of the organisation. All organisations are involved in some form of trade, and in the case of the public sector, this trade is usually a public service of some kind. The trading account is an income and expenditure account in relation to an organisation's trade. Where an organisation has many activities and sources of income and expenditure, the trading account differs from the organisation's main income and expenditure account in the following ways:

❖   It only reflects the income derived from the trade

❖   It only reflects the expenditure incurred in relation to the trade

Organisations that are multi-disciplinary may conduct several different trades and therefore may produce a separate trading account for each trade.

Some organisations often have a main trade which is composed of a number of different trades with other activities being peripheral. This is shown in the following table.

Organisation	Main Trade	Composite Trades	Other Activities
Local Authority	• Local public services	• Education • Social Services • Housing • Environment • Leisure, etc.	• Giving mortgages • Renting commercial property
Department of Transport	• Land, sea, air transport	• Railways • Highways • Road and vehicle safety • Shipping • Aviation etc.	• Grant giving • Research
Inland Revenue	• Collection of taxes	• Personal tax • Business tax • International tax • Valuations • Securities and investments, etc.	• Public relations • Education
Hospital	• Patient care	• Out patient • Surgery • In patient care and accommodation • Research and laboratory • Pharmacy, etc.	• Restaurant • Car park • Crèche

Trading accounts can be established for each of the individual components of the main trade, and even for some of the other activities that the organisation may undertake.

Preparing the Trading Account

As previously mentioned, the trading account is an income and expenditure account for the trade. In the public sector, the trade will most likely be a service, and often the income for the service comes from public funds, unlike a business whereby sales are usually made directly to third parties. In the case of the public sector, the direct beneficiaries of the trade often do not pay directly for the service.

Expenditure relating to the trade has to be recorded and set against the income from the trade. In order to calculate an accurate trading position it is important to match like with like, therefore if expenditure on a particular area relates to several trades it should be apportioned fairly between the trades and allocated to the correct trading account. This may be the case for expenditure items such as accommodation costs where accommodation is being shared between different trading activities.

An example of a local authority personnel department trading account is shown as follows:

	£	£
INCOME:		
Charges to Clients based on Time Sheets at £x per hour		
• Recharges to other departments		77,500
• Private Sector		45,000
• Voluntary Sector		40,000
• Advice to committee		5,000
		167,500
EXPENDITURE:		
Salaries	104,800	
Other Expenses	14,500	
Supplies and Services	8,700	
Controllable Expenditure	128,000	
SLA Costs	39,500	
(Share of costs charged by other departments allocated per number of staff)		167,500
Net Profit/Loss		NIL

The key to preparing a trading account is operating a good financial accounting system where expenditure and income items can be coded to the trade, and shared costs can be apportioned and allocated using fair criteria.

Objective of the Trading Account

The main objective is to measure the performance of the trade or service. In this case, performance is usually measured in financial terms in the form of the trading result, i.e. whether a surplus or deficit is achieved. Depending on the organisation's objectives, each trade may strive to break even where neither surplus nor deficit is desirable, otherwise there may be a desire to maximise surpluses or minimise deficits.

The performance achieved on the trading account can assist the organisation to answer the following questions:

Is the trade viable?

It is very important to establish if the trade can at least break even whereby the expenditure needed to deliver the service can be covered by the income generated by the service. If this is not the case, the organisation will have to consider to what extent it is prepared to support the trade from other funds.

Is the trade profitable?

If the trade generates surpluses, it can assist in compensating for deficits and overspending experienced by other parts of the organisation. Also, surpluses may be invested in service development.

Is the service an income generator?

The trading account will identify how much income can be generated by the trade. Generally, the income will tend to be externally supplied which may include grants, fees, charges, etc.

Is the trade suitable for competition?

The trading account will identify the nature of income and expenditure required by the service and hence whether or not it would be the type of service that might be attractive to third parties wishing to compete to deliver the service. Also, the trading account will assist the organisation to identify what changes need to be made in order to make the service suitable for competition. In the current climate of competitive tendering for public sector services, this question is being asked far more frequently.

SUMMARY

❏ The difference between the income and expenditure is either a surplus or a deficit

❏ Public sector organisations can derive income from a wide range of sources. These include grants, fees and charges, sales, interest, rents and dividends

❏ The income for a particular period relates to everything that has been earned in the period and does not necessarily equal the cash received

❏ Expenditure relates to what is used as opposed to the cash spent by the organisation

❏ Some of the main types of expenditure incurred by most organisations include employee costs, transport costs, supplies and services, accommodation costs, support service costs, and financing costs

❏ At the end of the accounting period, in order to obtain an accurate reflection of income and expenditure, adjustments may be made to take account of accruals, debtors, creditors, prepayments, depreciation and bad debts

❏ The key to preparing a trading account is operating a good financial accounting system

Exercise 4

Preparing a Trading Account

A new independent communications business unit comes into operation this year to provide communication services for which a separate trading account is required.

The cost of purchase and development of the appropriate equipment was £100,000 and a £100,000 loan was taken out to finance the purchase. The business unit provides a range of services which are sold to the public and private sectors.

Income for the first year included two contracts of £50,000 each from local authority departments and four contracts from DSOs and other business units averaging £20,000 each. The direct costs related to contract sales represents 25% of the contract price. At the end of the year all expenditure items had been paid for but 40% of the total contract fees due were outstanding.

The cost of running the unit is summarised as follows:

Consultant fees	£20,000
Salary of one manager and two assistants	£32,000
Salary of a part time administrative officer	£6,000
Office overheads	£6,000
Other charges	£5,000

Interest on the loan is 5% per annum payable by the end of the year, and depreciation has been set at 15% on equipment

From the information given, calculate the end of year trading account for the business unit, using the following pro forma.

	£	£
Income:		
Fees		
Expenditure:		
Direct costs		
Consultant fees		
Salaries		
Office overheads		
Other charges		
Loan interest		
Depreciation		
Total		
Surplus or Deficit for the year		

Suggested solutions to this exercise can be found on page 126

Exercise 5

Preparing an
Income and Expenditure Account

Using the proforma on page 33, calculate the income and expenditure account for Limit H.A. a housing association which has been developed as a result of a local authority stock transfer.

Limit H.A. has three trading accounts whose results are as follows:

	Housing Management Trading Account	Repairs and Maintenance Trading Account	Supported Housing Trading Account
Income	£1,200,000	£300,000	£450,000
Less: Expenditure	£1,100,000	£305,000	£480,000
Surplus/Deficit	£100,000	-£5,000	-£30,000

In addition, Limit H.A. earned £15,000 interest from bank deposits, and paid £65,000 in interest on loans owed by the organisation. There were central costs of £45,000 not allocated to specific trading accounts, and depreciation for the year was £10,000.

Limit H.A.
Income and Expenditure Account
for the year ended 19XX

£

Income

Expenditure

Surplus/Deficit

Suggested solutions to this exercise can be found on page 127

Exercise 6

Preparing Your Own Trading Account

Prepare a draft trading account for your own section within your organisation. (This could be either a division, business unit, cost centre, etc.)

Calculate your income   [   ] A
Recharges to other departments, external
fees, etc.

Identify all areas of expenditure

_____	_____
_____	_____
_____	_____
_____	_____
_____	_____
_____	_____
_____	_____
_____	_____
_____	_____
_____	_____

TOTAL   [   ] B

+ Surplus/- Deficit for the year   [   ] A-B

Remember income includes everything earned during the year, regardless of whether the cash had been received or not, and expenditure includes everything used during the year regardless of whether it has been paid for or not.

Chapter 4

THE BALANCE SHEET

The Balance Sheet

Many people can understand the workings of the income and expenditure account and trading account, however the balance sheet often remains a mystery. In order to fully understand financial accounts, it is essential to understand both financial statements. A proforma balance sheet was set out in chapter 2. The key thing to remember is that the balance sheet is a statement of assets and liabilities and the two sides must always balance. In other words:

$$\boxed{\text{Assets}} \quad = \quad \boxed{\text{Liabilities}}$$

remembering that assets are owned by the organisation and liabilities are owed by the organisation to someone else.

Types of Asset

There are a number of different types of assets which fall into the following categories:

Fixed Assets
Intangible Assets
Current Assets

There are many other types of assets that are mentioned from time to time but they are usually just alternative names for one of the three mentioned above. Each type of asset is discussed in the following paragraphs.

Fixed Assets

The most well known assets are those which are referred to in the balance sheet proforma as fixed assets. These include land and buildings, equipment, fixtures and fittings, vehicles and plant and machinery.

All these items have an ongoing value to the organisation in so far as they will last within the organisation for more than one year. How long these items will last varies considerably from one organisation to another and each organisation will adopt depreciation policies with respect to how long they expect the fixed asset to last. For example, if it is assumed that vehicles will last for 4 years, then it is normal for them to be depreciated over 4 years. One approach to depreciation is to take a straight line approach and depreciate the asset by 25% each year. Alternatively, the depreciation charge may be calculated based on the reducing balance of the asset value each year.

For example, if a car was purchased for £12,000 and assumed to last the organisation 4 years, adopting the straight line approach, each year £3,000 would be written off the value of the car as depreciation. This would be shown as a depreciation charge in the income and expenditure account and each year be reflected in the balance sheet as a reduction in the vehicle's value.

Year	Vehicle Cost	Depreciation charge for the year	Accumulated Depreciation	Net Book Value
Year 1	12,000	3,000	3,000	9,000
Year 2	12,000	3,000	6,000	6,000
Year 3	12,000	3,000	9,000	3,000
Year 4	12,000	3,000	12,000	0

Different items in the organisation's fixed asset portfolio will attract different levels of depreciation. The level of depreciation charged will be the subject of the organisation's depreciation policy.

It is normal practice to state all assets in the accounts at their original cost at the time of acquisition. The actual value of the asset will change over time, and it is often considered that depreciation reflects the diminishing value that most assets have after they have been used. The calculation of depreciation is far from an exact science and is often only an estimate of the decline in value. It is only if and when an asset is sold that some idea of its true value can be established.

Some assets increase in value over time. Traditionally it has been assumed that land and buildings appreciate in value rather than depreciate over time and hence, these tend not to be depreciated. The balance sheet will only reflect current values if they are re-valued from time to time. It is quite common for some organisations to have their land and buildings revalued every five or ten years to take account of the current market place, and the appreciation or depreciation that may have occurred in values.

Fixed assets are sometimes referred to as capital assets because they are a result of capital expenditure. When an organisation purchases an asset that has an ongoing value, it is usually capitalised, i.e. forms part of the fixed assets in the balance sheet. Other expenditure relates to revenue items which are reflected in the income and expenditure account. Revenue items are "written off" during the year because they have been used up in providing the organisation's services.

Intangible Assets

Intangible assets are those which have no physical existence. They include items such as goodwill, the premium or excess value over and above the tangible worth of the organisation which a buyer is prepared to pay. It also includes items such as brand names, patents and trademarks. The valuation of intangible assets is often very subjective and therefore the accounting approach to these assets is to treat them prudently and to exclude them from the balance sheet as much as possible.

Current Assets

Unlike fixed assets, which generally are expected to stay within the organisation for at least a year, current assets by their nature are very changeable and do vary regularly within a year. The main types of current assets are:

❖ Stocks; e.g. stationery, food stocks, materials; all of which alter on a regular basis

❖ Debtors; amounts owing from customers. Receipts can be obtained almost daily, hence, debtors go down, also invoicing can be carried out daily, hence, the value of debtors go up

❖ Bank and cash balances; again, cash receipts and payments can be made daily, hence, cash balances fluctuate up and down accordingly

Liabilities

Liabilities represent everything that the organisation owes and are generally split between long and short term liabilities.

❖ Long term liabilities are those that generally speaking will be outstanding for more than a year. For example:

~ Loans
~ Mortgages
~ Hire purchase agreements
~ Leases, etc.

❖ Short term liabilities are those which are generally repayable within a year. They primarily comprise of creditors and bank overdrafts. Creditors refer to the whole range of payments payable within the year such as:

~ Rents,
~ Salaries,
~ Interest charges,
~ Suppliers,
~ Loan repayments,
~ Professional fees, etc.

Bank overdrafts are a short term liability as they are repayable on demand

Another important liability is any kind of investment made by the owners of an organisation, normally in the form of share capital. The reason why share capital is a liability is because it represents an investment into the organisation by the "owners" of the organisation and is therefore **owed** by the organisation to the owners.

In many private sector organisations, share capital often represents a large injection of funds necessary to provide investment or working capital. When used in the public sector, however, share capital is often a nominal amount to reflect ownership. For example, it is quite common for the executive or management committee members to hold say nominal £1 shares in the organisation to reflect their "ownership" or legal "connection" to the organisation.

Reserves

In whatever form they are represented, the total reserves represent the "net worth of the organisation". Each year's surpluses are added to the previous years accumulated reserves to arrive at the accumulated reserves for the current year. Similarly, any deficits are deducted from reserves and will reduce the level of accumulated reserves. Reserves are shown on the liability side of the balance sheet as shown below:

Assets		
Fixed	X	
Current	X	
Total Assets	**X**	A
Liabilities		
Owners/Shareholders Funds	X	
Long Term	X	
Short Term	X	
Reserves	X	
Total Liabilities	**X**	B
A = B		

Other items with a similar status to reserves are listed as follows:

General Fund
A term used for accumulated surpluses

Capital Funds
Reserves earmarked for specific future capital expenditure

Owners Equity
Amounts invested by individuals in a private business

Share Capital
Amounts invested by stakeholders in an organisation which is limited by shares. These companies can be profit making or not-for-profit, but both types have limited liability.

Unlike loans, which are "owed" to the bank, reserves and similar items are "owed" to the "owners" of the organisation. In the case of a company, the owners would be the shareholders, whereas for a local authority the owners would be the council tax payers, and for a voluntary organisation it would be the trustees or members.

The surplus or deficit made each year is the main figure that links together the income and expenditure account and the balance sheet. The surplus shown on the income and expenditure account reflects the results of the organisation's performance for the year which is "owed to" the owners of the organisation, hence it is represented as a liability on the balance sheet.

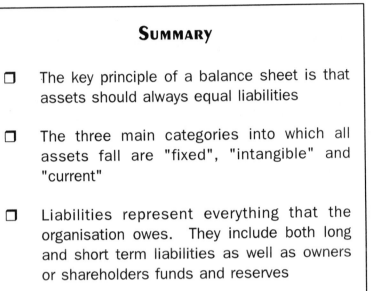

SUMMARY

❐ The key principle of a balance sheet is that assets should always equal liabilities

❐ The three main categories into which all assets fall are "fixed", "intangible" and "current"

❐ Liabilities represent everything that the organisation owes. They include both long and short term liabilities as well as owners or shareholders funds and reserves

Exercise 7

Understanding Assets and Liabilities

Make a list of all the assets and liabilities that your service area uses (even if it does not own them) and estimate their value.

Assets	£	Liabilities *	£
Total A		**Total B**	

* Note: Reserves should be on this side although you may not be able to establish a realistic estimate for this item.

Undertake the following net worth calculation: A-B = ☐

Exercise 8

Calculating the Balance Sheet

Using the information in exercise 4, calculate the balance sheet for the Communications Business Unit using the proforma on the next page:

Suggested solutions to this exercise can be found on page 128

Communications Business Unit
Balance Sheet

	Cost £	Depreciation £	NBV £	
Fixed Assets				
Equipment	☐	☐	☐	A
Current Assets				
Debtors	☐			
Cash	☐			
(sub total x)		☐		
Current Liabilities				
Creditors	☐			
Overdraft	☐			
(sub total y)		☐		
Net Current Assets (x-y)			☐	B
Net Assets			☐	A+B
Represented by				
Surplus for the year from the trading account		☐		
Loan		☐		
(A+B) should equal C			☐	C

Chapter 5

KEY FINANCIAL PERFORMANCE INDICATORS

There are a number of financial indicators that can be beneficial in identifying an organisation's performance. Most indicators are compared with either a target for the current or previous years to indicate increasing or decreasing performance. In this chapter we discuss some of the key indicators which are used by many organisations on a regular basis and are of most use to public sector managers.

Level of Surpluses

Within private organisations reference is often made to "the bottom line"; this means the organisation's level of profits or profitability. For companies this is one of the most important measures of their performance. Within the public sector, the bottom line refers to the surplus or deficit made. This measure is also important within a public sector context, however, the level of importance will vary with each organisation's objectives. For example, some public sector organisations have an objective to ensure that all their income is utilised during the year and therefore aim for a break-even position, whereby there are neither surpluses or deficits. Others will have targets for surpluses to be made in order to build up reserves or funds for the future.

The surplus or deficit achieved by the organisation is identified on the income and expenditure account produced at various stages during the year or at the end of the year. Individual activities within the organisation may produce separate trading accounts which will show the surplus or deficit for that activity. Remember:

| Income | - | Expenditure | = | Surplus or Deficit |

One way in which surpluses can be used as an indicator is to compare the actual surplus achieved with the budgeted surplus. Budgets will often be developed on a break even basis. A surplus will only result if the actual income exceeds the actual expenditure incurred. This occurs if more income is received than planned, or more usually, expenditure is below that budgeted. In some cases a surplus is not a positive performance indicator as it may reflect a reduction in the level of service delivered. Similarly, deficits may not necessarily be a negative indicator if they are supported by uncontrollable circumstances leading to increased levels of service delivery.

An example is given as follows:

Budgeted surplus for the year	£2,000
Actual surplus for the year	£1,500
Under-achievement	£500 or 25%

This shows performance as being 25% below target calculated as:

$$\frac{\text{Actual Surplus} - \text{Budgeted Surplus}}{\text{Budgeted Surplus}} \times 100\%$$

A further use of surplus as a performance measure is to make a comparison with the previous year, for example:

	This Year (£)	Previous Year (£)	Percentage Increase/ Decrease
Actual Surplus	1,500	1,000	50%
Budgeted Surplus	2,000	1,500	33%
Over/Under Achievement	-500	-500	0
Percentage	-25%	-33%	8%

This table of figures shows that in both years there has been an underachievement with respect to reaching the surplus performance targets. The monetary value of the under-performance has been £500 in both cases, but as the targets for each year were different, it represents a different rate of under-performance. The previous year was 33% below target whereas this year's performance was only 25% below target. The actual surplus achieved this year shows a 50% increase on the previous year, whereas the budgeted growth in surplus was only 33%. In summary, it is clear that although the performance target was not achieved in either year, this year there was an overall 8% increase in performance compared with the previous year.

The above analysis demonstrates that figures can be manipulated to show a positive or a negative performance, i.e. it could be said that performance has been poor because this year's result was 25% below target, or it could be said that this year's performance has been good as there has been a 50% growth in surplus compared with last year and an 8% overall increase in relative performance.

Rate of Return

The rate of return has always been an important measure in the private sector, and refers to the "return" on "investment" (ROI) or the "return" on "capital employed" (ROCE). The definitions of "investment" and "capital employed" can and do vary from organisation to organisation, however usual definitions include the following:

Net Assets

This figure is clearly stated on the organisation's balance sheet and takes into account fixed assets and net current assets.

Owners Investment and Long Term Loans

This figure tends to be equivalent to the net asset figure

Owners Investment Only

This figure will include any direct investment made by the owners of the organisation and any accumulated reserves and special funds. It does not take into account any debt being used by the organisation for its operations

Capital Assets Only

This figure includes only the fixed assets

For the purpose of this text, we will define capital employed as being equivalent to net assets.

In the public sector, this measure has also become very important, particularly in the case of local authorities. Since the introduction of Compulsory Competitive Tendering (CCT), any local authority that wins a bid in-house has to achieve a rate of return set by the government. If this rate of return is not achieved then the government can determine whether or not the in-house provider, usually referred to as a Direct Labour or Service Organisation, should continue to deliver the contract or whether the contract should be re-tendered.

The rate of return achieved by any trading activity is important because it reflects the rate of income generated by a particular investment. If a trading activity's return on capital is less than that which could be achieved by investing the money in a bank or building society (i.e. a safe investment) then it may be considered unwise to take the risk and invest in the trade. Therefore, the target rate of return for a trading activity is usually set at a higher level than the ruling average rate of interest in order to reflect the risk. Most commercial companies establish their own internal rate of return reflecting their attitude to risk taking, particularly for new ventures.

With respect to local authority compulsory competitive tendering, the government has set a rate of return which reflects the average interest rates of the day.

The rate of return is calculated using the following formula:

$$\frac{\text{Profit or Surplus}}{\text{Capital Employed}} \quad \times \quad 100\%$$

An example of this calculation is set out as follows:

A personnel division within a local authority has been established as a business unit in preparation for the competitive tendering of the whole service. In order to deliver the service, the following capital is required:

	£
Computer equipment	10,000
Office fixtures and fittings	4,000
Working capital*	6,000
TOTAL	£20,000

* This figure represents the capital needed to fund day to day operations due to the usual difference in timing between receiving the cash income and making payments for expenditure items. E.g. rent usually needs to be paid in advance. In the private sector this is often represented by an overdraft, in the public sector it is not usually so clear cut as each business unit does not have its own bank account.

After a year of trading, the Personnel Business Unit achieved the following:

	£
Income	400,000
Less:	
Expenditure	390,400
Surplus	600

The return on capital employed for the business unit is calculated by dividing the surplus achieved for the year by the capital employed by the unit, i.e. the original £20,000.

$$\text{Rate of Return} \quad \frac{600}{20,000} \quad \times \quad 100\% \quad = \quad 3\%$$

Depending on the organisation's objectives, 3% may or may not be a satisfactory level of performance. For example, if it was essential for the personnel business unit to achieve a 6% rate of return, the level of surplus would be insufficient. If a target rate of return has been set and the capital employed known (or well estimated) at the beginning of the year, then a target for the level of surplus can be set. In this case the target would have been £1,200 if 6% is the target rate of return.

In many cases public sector activities could be assumed to have nil capital employed as all assets are rented and an "asset rent" is charged to the trading account. In such cases a return on capital employed would also be nil therefore the trading account need only break-even.

Level of Liquidity

The level of liquidity is a performance measure reflecting the day to day efficiency in managing the organisation's cash flow. Liquidity levels are calculated by comparing the current assets with the current liabilities, i.e.

Current assets ⇨ including stock, debtors and cash
Current liabilities ⇨ including creditors and overdrafts

Within the public sector, the level of liquidity is often far removed from individual operational units, and is controlled centrally. Most public sector organisations, as with the private sector, will have timing differences with respect of cash receipts and cash payments which have to be managed. If an organisation becomes illiquid it means that it will have difficulty in making payments as and when they became due. This can often arise if a great deal of cash is tied up in the form of debtors and hence cash balances are too low to pay all the outstanding creditors. In order to assist with this, many organisations will arrange overdraft facilities with their bankers.

There are two commonly used ratios to measure the liquidity of any organisation, these are defined as follows:

The "liquidity ratio":

$$\frac{\text{Current Assets}}{\text{Current Liabilities}}$$

This ratio should be in excess of 1.5 to demonstrate adequate liquidity.

The "quick ratio", or "acid test" is a similar ratio:

$$\frac{\text{Current Assets - Stock}}{\text{Current Liabilities}}$$

This ratio reflects only the cash and near cash current assets (i.e. debtors). Most public sector organisations have very little stock and therefore the quick ratio and liquidity ratio will more or less be the same.

This measure of performance particularly reflects the way in which an organisation manages it's cash, a vital asset. The direct cost of mis-management is the cost of having to use an overdraft - interest charged, or the lost interest on cash deposits. As public sector services become more commercialised, liquidity will increasingly become more important when assessing performance.

Other Financial Indicators

There are other financial indicators which may be used to assess the financial performance of an organisation. The indicators identified below are most regularly used by the private sector, although still have relevance for public sector organisations.

Debtor Days

Number of days taken for debt collection from those who owe the organisation money. This is calculated in the following way. Firstly the debtors turnover ratio is calculated by dividing credit sales (those where customers are given time to pay) by the value of the outstanding debtors at the year end:

$$\frac{\text{Credit Sales}}{\text{Year End Debtors}} = \text{Debtors Turnover Ratio}$$

This ratio is then divided into 365 days:

$$\frac{365 \text{ days}}{\text{Debtors Turnover Ratio}}$$

Ideally this should be no longer than 30 days. Longer collection periods may contribute to cash flow problems. This ratio is useful to calculate in relation to items such as rent collection, where the value of rents is divided by the year end rent arrears to calculate the rent turnover ratio, then divide the ratio into 365 days to calculate the average number of days to collect the rent:

Gearing

This relates to the level of long term debt used by the organisation. It is calculated using the following formula:

$$\frac{\text{Debt Level}}{\text{Net Assets}} \quad x \quad 100\%$$

Depending on the type of activity undertaken by the organisation, high levels of debt may indicate poor performance. In addition, high levels of debts will require a high level of revenue to support the resulting interest payments.

For the public sector the financial indicators of performance will tend to concentrate more on the following:

❖ Rate of increase or decrease in expenditure

❖ Level of variance between actual and budgeted income and expenditure

❖ Level, rate and timing of income collection such as rent arrears for local authorities

SUMMARY

☐ Within the public sector, the bottom line refers to the surplus or deficit made at the end of an accounting period. The desired level of surplus will vary from one organisation to another

☐ The rate of return has always been an important measure in the private sector and has become increasingly important within the public sector. This is particularly the case for local authorities who under CCT are required to meet a rate of return set by the government

☐ The level of liquidity is a performance measure reflecting the day to day efficiency in managing the organisation's cash flow

☐ Other financial indicators which may be used to assess the financial performance of an organisation include debtor days and gearing

Exercise 9

Calculating Key Financial Ratios

The legal services business unit of a local authority have produced the following financial accounting information for the last two years.

```
┌─────────────────────────────────────────────────────────────┐
│                    TRADING ACCOUNTS                          │
│                                                              │
│                              Year 1        Year 2            │
│                                £             £               │
│                                                              │
│  INCOME                                                      │
│    Fees - internal recharges  500,000       550,000         │
│    Fees - external work        100,000       150,000         │
│  Total                         600,000       700,000         │
│                                                              │
│  EXPENDITURE                                                 │
│    Salaries                   400,000       440,000         │
│    Supplies and services       80,000       100,000         │
│    Overheads                   50,000        80,000         │
│    Recharges                   54,000        63,000         │
│  Total                         584,000       683,000         │
│                                                              │
│  Surplus for the year         £16,000       £17,000         │
└─────────────────────────────────────────────────────────────┘
```

In addition, the business unit used £100,000 worth of assets in the business both years.

a) **Calculate the following ratios which represent financial performance**

	Year 1	Year 2
Return on Capital Employed		
Surplus as a percentage of income		
Income growth year on year		

b) **What other information would you wish to have in order to assess the business unit's performance over the two years.**

....
....
....
....
....
....
....
....
....

Suggested solutions to this exercise can be found on page 130

Exercise 10

Interpretation of Financial Ratios

Two local health centres have been asked to provide some financial statistics which set out their respective financial performance for last year. The figures given are as follows:

	Health Centre 1	Health Centre 2
• Surplus for the year	£5,000	£600
• Surplus as a percentage of total income	1%	0.2%
• Return on capital	10%	2.5%
• Liquidity ratio	1	2
• Debtors level as a percentage of total income	30%	20%
• Debtor days	110 days	73 days
• Percentage variance on surplus (actual compared with budget)	-50%	-10%
• Increase in productivity	0.5%	6%

From the above information, you have been asked to give your interpretation of the figures and advise which one of the health centres should close.

Suggested solutions to this exercise can be found on page 131

Chapter 6

THE IMPORTANCE OF CASH FLOW

How Cash is used in the Organisation?

All organisations have to undertake transactions in order to engage in any kind of trade. Goods have to be purchased, staff have to be paid, and therefore cash is essential if an organisation is to operate and survive. All organisations have cash receipts from a variety of sources, e.g. grants, fees, rents, etc. and cash payments for a variety of different purposes related to its activities. This incoming and outgoing of cash is generally referred to as the cash flow. In addition to the conduct of transactions, cash has many uses in the organisation. These are:

Investment

Cash can be invested in terms of bank deposits or be used to purchase other items which can be used as an investment for the organisation. Investments usually yield a "return". For example, in the case of a bank deposit the return takes the form of interest, whilst in the case of an investment in shares the return would be the dividend.

Provisions

Similar to insurance, it may be necessary to make a provision for a one-off event that will happen in the future, for example, there may be a need to make redundancies. Cash balances can therefore be set aside in order to meet future redundancy payments.

Cash is usually part of every transaction with the exception of certain accounting adjustments for which there are no cash implications, e.g. depreciation, bad debt write offs, and so on.

Timing of Cash Flows

The timing of incoming and outgoing cash is important if one is to manage cash balances, and there are a number of reasons why the cash balance needs to be managed. Some of the key reasons are summarised as follows:

Limited or no overdraft facilities:

If an organisation has an overdraft facility it is usually limited to a maximum amount and cash balances must be maintained within this overdraft limit. Some organisations have no overdraft facilities as bankers are perhaps not prepared to take the risk of this type of lending. This is especially true of many smaller voluntary sector organisations, which often deliver services on behalf of larger public sector bodies, such as health trusts, and local authorities.

Minimising costs:

If cash balances are depleted and overdrafts are used there will be a cost implication. Most overdrafts carry a high rate of interest and therefore careful cash management can minimise the amount and the frequency of overdraft use and hence minimise cost.

Maximising income:

Surplus cash balances are usually invested, this is discussed in more detail under treasury management. However, careful cash management will result in more cash being available for investment and hence higher earnings.

Reputation:

Poor cash management can result in the organisation not being able to make payments when they are due. This leads to a poor image with suppliers if they have to wait over the due date for payment. It may even lead to suppliers ceasing to make supplies to the organisation, or withdrawing credit and hence requiring cash on delivery. Not having credit terms with suppliers can severely affect cash flows as cash has to be paid out immediately instead of after 30 or 60 days (the usual credit terms offered by suppliers).

Going concern:

If the organisation is to remain a going concern and not face the possibility of closure it has to have sufficient cash available to make its payments when they fall due. If cash becomes a severe problem it can go beyond a poor reputation with suppliers. It may lead to suppliers taking legal action and ultimately forcing closure of the organisation. Further if salaries are not paid, employees could withdraw their labour and again the organisation would have to close.

The timing of incoming and outgoing cash flows can be affected by a number of factors as shown in the following table:

Source of Cash In	Factors Affecting Timing
Grants	Much of the public sector is funded by grants. The timing of it's receipt may be affected by the speed at which claims are submitted, or by the efficiency or otherwise of the grant giver in processing the claim. It is usual for an annual grant to be received in phases over the year, e.g. quarterly. Cash flows are particularly affected if grants are received in advance or in arrear. It can mean the difference of several months of having either a positive cash balance or a negative one.
Fees/Charges/ Sales	As with commercial organisations, the public sector sometimes transacts with the general public or other bodies whereby a sale is made or a fee charged. For example, local authorities raise some of their income from levying local taxes. These charges have to be collected. Cash flows are affected by the speed at which cash is received. Getting people to pay quickly can be difficult, and it is often normal to offer payment arrangements and credit terms. The timing of receipts from third parties will depend on the efficiency with which the organisation implements its collections policies. These policies may include incentives for early payers such as discounts, and legal action against non-payment.
Rents	It is usual to require a tenant to pay their rent in advance. In the case of commercial buildings, rents are usually paid quarterly, whereas for residential lettings rents are paid weekly or monthly. Even though a rent may be levied in advance it does not mean that the cash is received on the due date. Again, collections policies will affect how quickly cash is received.
Interest	Interest is earned on cash deposits if they are invested properly. Often a current account balance does not attract interest. This is where treasury management will affect the amount of cash received from this source and its timing. Treasury management is discussed in the next section.
Loans	This is a source of cash which tends to be a one off event. It will usually relate to a specific activity such as the purchase of a property. It is not uncommon within the private sector for a company to take out a loan to assist day to day working capital, especially in a development stage. The factors affecting timing include when the loan can be drawn down whether all at once or in phases, and how the loan money is to be used within the organisation.

Source of Cash Out	Factors Affecting Timing
Salaries	These payments have to be made regularly, usually at the end of a month or a week depending on the terms and conditions by which staff are employed. Due to the nature of these payments, there is little that will affect the timing of this particular cash outgoing. In some organisations bonuses are paid, this can be a drain on cash resources, but the timing of such payments may be dictated by pre set in-house rules and procedures, or there may be considerable flexibility.
Suppliers	There are many factors that affect the timing of these payments. It is usually to an organisation's advantage to delay paying suppliers for as long as possible to obtain a cash flow advantage. Most suppliers will offer credit terms, particularly to established organisations. These terms usually allow a number of days to pay, e.g. 14 or 30 days is quite common. Organisations often exceed this number of days depending on their existing cash balances. A small supplier has little bargaining power with a large customer, and sometimes the organisation can dictate the payment terms. As public sector organisations have a public image, most will try and adhere to the suppliers credit terms. On the other hand suppliers may offer discounts for prompt payment, and this may affect the timing of payment.
Rents	The timing of these payments will be dictated by the lease agreement. It is normal for rents to be paid in advance.
Interest	The timing of interest payments can often be negotiated with the lender. It is in the interest of the organisation to arrange for interest payments to be made flexibly, however it is usual for the payment dates to be fixed after the initial negotiations have taken place.
Loans to third parties	Loans are made at the organisation's discretion and hence the timing at which cash goes out in this manner can be closely controlled. It is usual for a repayment schedule to be given to the borrower, along with interest charges, such that incoming cash flows can also be predicted. However, there will be a risk in lending in so far as the borrower may not be able to repay.

In order to assist with cash flow management and the timing of cash flows it is normal to produce a cash flow forecast each year and to use this as a monitoring tool. The cash flow forecast is discussed in detail in the next chapter.

Treasury Management

This is the term given to the cash management function in an organisation. The point of this is to maximise the income that can be generated from cash and to minimise the cost of using cash. Effective treasury management will depend on the investment and borrowing strategies used by the organisation. For some public sector bodies these will be limited by legislation, for example levels of borrowing may be restricted or the types of investment that can be made limited to risk free investments.

Investment strategies

Key investment strategies have been identified as follows:

❖ Keep current account balances to a minimum and invest surplus cash in a deposit account, even if only for overnight.

❖ Depending on the amounts of cash available, longer term investments can be considered. The length of time for which cash can be tied up in a longer term investment will be dictated by the cash flow forecast which will indicate when cash is required by the organisation.

❖ Risk is related to reward so the investment strategy should be developed based on the level of risk the organisation is prepared to take. If it is a low risk strategy then investments will be limited to bank deposits, treasury bonds with a fixed return, and so on. Investments in stocks and shares have a higher degree of risk but scope for greater returns.

❖   All interest rates should be negotiated in order to achieve the highest rates possible. Interest rates change every day and hence they need to be monitored closely. The person responsible for treasury management should try a range of alternative sources in the market place in order to achieve the highest rates.

Borrowing strategies

There are many different types of borrowing, but all have a cost. There is short term borrowing and long term borrowing. Short term is usually more expensive and volatile, whereas long term is cheaper and more secure. Treasury management activities concentrate on providing for the day to day cash needs of the organisation and planning to ensure that future cash requirements can be met.

❖   The borrowing strategy may be affected by internal policies with respect to borrowing which may limit the amounts that can be borrowed, and the lending organisations that can be used.

❖   The treasury manager will seek to minimise the cost of any type of borrowing that is undertaken. This may result in a need to shop around in the market place to obtain the best rates.

❖ By preparing a cash flow forecast, it will be clear as to when there might be a potential need to acquire extra cash and hence borrowing facilities should be arranged well in advance.

Cash balances should be monitored on a daily basis as they will change every day. The person responsible for treasury management will then have to make an appropriate decision as to how to invest surplus cash or how cash short falls should be funded.

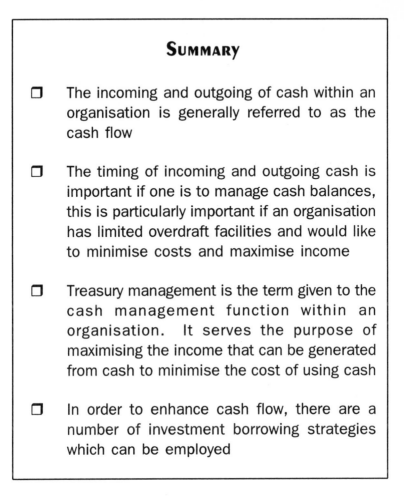

SUMMARY

❑ The incoming and outgoing of cash within an organisation is generally referred to as the cash flow

❑ The timing of incoming and outgoing cash is important if one is to manage cash balances, this is particularly important if an organisation has limited overdraft facilities and would like to minimise costs and maximise income

❑ Treasury management is the term given to the cash management function within an organisation. It serves the purpose of maximising the income that can be generated from cash to minimise the cost of using cash

❑ In order to enhance cash flow, there are a number of investment borrowing strategies which can be employed

Exercise 11

Understanding Your Cash Flow

Complete the following questionnaire

1) **Where does your cash come from?**

      a) Grant (50% - 75%) ❑

      b) Grant (excess of 75%) ❑

      c) Fees/earned income excess of 50% ❑

      d) Total mixture, or varies each year ❑

2) **Does your organisation have an overdraft facility?**

      a) Yes ❑

      b) No ❑

3) **Is there anyone in the organisation responsible for treasury management?**

      a) Yes ❑

      b) No ❑

4) **Do creditors ever ring up asking for their money?**

      a) Yes ❑

      b) No ❑

      c) Sometimes ❑

5) **Are salaries paid regularly and on time?**

    a) Yes   ❑

    b) Sometimes   ❑

    c) No   ❑

6) **Are there ever freezes on expenditure during the year?**

    a) No   ❑

    b) sometimes   ❑

    c) Yes   ❑

7) **Do a lot of people owe the organisation money?**

    a) Yes   ❑

    b) No   ❑

8) **Does the organisation have high finance costs?**

    a) Yes   ❑

    b) No   ❑

9) **Does the organisation have interest income?**

    a) Yes   ❑

    b) No   ❑

10) **Calculate the liquidity ratio for the organisation (net assets/net liabilities). Is it...**

    a) Under 1?   ❑

    b) Between 1 and 2?   ❑

    c) Over 2?   ❑

For scoring results see suggested solutions on page 132

Chapter 7

FINANCIAL PLANNING AND CONTROL

Financial planning involves looking ahead at all the organisation's financial requirements and identifying how they can be met over the time horizon being considered. The financial requirements should be based on the organisation's business plan objectives, hence linked directly to service delivery.

The financial plan will identify the level of income required to meet the expenditure needs of the organisation for both revenue and capital items, and also where that income will be obtained. The plan will also consider the cash flow implications of the expected timing of receipts and payments, and hence the need for additional cash resources at particular times.

In order to control finances, there needs to be an initial plan otherwise there is no benchmark against which to measure performance over the year. Control therefore has to be within a framework which is set by the financial plan.

The financial planning process should include the following stages:

- Setting the objectives for the organisation

- Identifying and forecasting the expenditure levels needed to deliver those objectives

- Identifying and forecasting the income sources available to fund the expenditure

- Identifying and forecasting the timing of cash flows, and resulting cash requirements

Each stage of the process is discussed in detail in the following paragraphs.

Setting Objectives

Most organisations undertake a process of setting objectives. In some cases this is part of a business or service planning process. In any event, public sector organisations should set targets with respect to service delivery for the future. These plans will usually cover at least one year, or perhaps a longer period. Objectives will identify the type, quality and quantity of service to be provided.

Forecasting Expenditure

Having set the objectives, it is up to the organisation to determine the level of expenditure required in order to deliver those services. Depending on the organisational structure, expenditure forecasts may be prepared by divisions, business units, service cost centres, etc. The forecast will consider how much needs to be spent on each area of expenditure each month. An example of how these figures are constructed is shown as follows:

Key Expenditure Headings	Process for developing forecast figures
Salaries	This will be based on the number of staff employed and current salaries, the terms and conditions of employment, the level of increments, pay awards, and bonuses. It should also reflect known potential joiners and leavers during the year. For example, if there is currently a vacant post, the forecast for the following year should reflect the timing of when that post will be filled. Salaries will be paid monthly (wages perhaps weekly) and the forecast should reflect the level of expected payment each month taking into account the changes to the salary levels that will occur throughout the year.
Other Employment Costs	Some staff may have additional payments made which are not directly related to the salary. These may include things such as a car allowance, or a child care allowance. Other costs will also include the employers national insurance contributions, pension contributions and other payments made on behalf of employees such as subscriptions to professional organisations. All these payments should be subject to accurate forecasting.
Transport	This forecast should be based upon the number and type of vehicles used and the average cost per journey. Previous year statistics will prove a useful starting point. These vehicles may include taxis, coaches, leased cars, etc. Not all journeys can be planned and therefore it may be sensible to add some contingency allowance to this budget for unforeseen uses of transport.
Accommodation	Accommodation costs such as rent are usually fixed for a number of years, giving a set charge for the year paid either quarterly or monthly and hence the expenditure can be accurately forecast. Even if a move is to be made, these are usually planned in advance and the new rents known well in advance. Other accommodation costs will vary from year to year, however these can still be forecast accurately by taking the actual charge for the current year and agreeing a rate of increase with the service provider - usually to reflect inflation.

Key Expenditure Headings	Process for developing forecast figures
Supplies and Services	This is probably one of the most difficult areas to forecast as it is difficult to predict what goods and services may be required during the year. However, the data that should be used in order to achieve accurate forecasting include the following: • the detailed action plan for the year • the planned expenditure for the year, for which estimates should be sought from suppliers • from the previous year, the profile and nature of expenditure, and the list of unplanned expenditure, identifying which items were one-off, and which items are likely to recur • the level of variance experienced in the previous year for each area of expenditure The monthly forecast will reflect the peaks and troughs in the different areas of expenditure, and guess work should be kept to a minimum, i.e. figures should be developed on sound assumptions.
Support Service Costs	Depending on the nature of the organisation, support services, such as legal, finance, and personnel may be supplied by in-house departments, or by third party contractors. In any event, when developing the forecast, ideally an estimate of these costs for the year should be gained from the service provider, along with the method of payment. These estimates should be subject to negotiation such that the best rates are obtained.
Finance costs	These costs reflect the cost of borrowing, this may include a loan or the use of overdraft facilities. Within the public sector, these costs are often unknown until the end of the year and hence are difficult to forecast. It is important that a figure is given for these costs for completeness. A starting point for the forecast will be to take last years figures along with the predicted interest rates.
Other expenditure	There will be other expenditure items which do not fit strictly into any of the previous categories. On the whole the best way to forecast these are to use prior year profiles of expenditure for similar items, or to obtain estimates from suppliers and providers for new items. It is usually prudent to include a miscellaneous, or contingency sum in a forecast to take account of miscalculation and unforeseen expenditure items.

For most public sector organisations, staffing will be the main area of expenditure.

Forecasting Income

Depending on the source of income, developing a forecast for income can be far more difficult than forecasting expenditure. The receipt of grants may be predicted, and once agreed a payment schedule is usually given. However, income from charges, fees, and so on can be very difficult to predict as fee levels will be determined by demand. All forecasts require assumptions to be made, and income forecasts require assumptions to be as prudent as possible because unlike expenditure which can be subject to a certain amount of internal control, income is often subject to external forces.

The following table gives examples of how income forecasts can be developed for the most typical sources of income within public sector organisations:

Key Income Headings	Process for developing forecast figures
Grants	The most difficult aspect of forecasting grants is knowing the level of grant that will be given in a particular year. Often grant givers do not determine the level of grants until very near the beginning of the year in question. This is the case for both central and local government. Therefore forecasting income can be delayed due to a very important but unknown figure. To assist with the process, an estimate should be made of grant income based on previous year levels, inflation rates, and any known changes that have been made. A prudent approach should be taken with respect to specific grants, which should only be included in the forecast if agreed. These grants will usually be matched with expenditure and hence there should be a nil effect on the overall net position of the forecast.

Key Income Headings	Process for developing forecast figures
Fees and Charges	Many public sector organisations charge a fee for some of the services they provide, or levy a charge. Where these services are demand led, forecasting the level of income from these sources is extremely difficult. It relies upon an accurate forecast of prospective demand over the forecast period, along with the mix of services that will be used. Such figures can be obtained by undertaking research into future trends, and analysing historic trends. If there is no available data any estimates of such income should be very prudent, and reflect the lowest levels of expectation. Fees to be generated under contract are more straight forward as they should be agreed in advance with the service user/customer. For example, a local education authority payroll service may have contracts to deliver payroll services to grant maintained schools.
Sales	Sales tend to refer to products as opposed to services where the term fee is more common. Forecasting sales has the same difficulties as mentioned above for fees and charges.
Rent	Some organisations have a limited supply of properties from which they can generate rents. This allows for accurate forecasting of rental income, as each unit will tend to have a fixed rent or rent increases will be set in advance.
Interest	Income arising from investments will vary depending on the level of investments made. Long term investments will often have a fixed rate of return or be linked to variable bank interest rates which can be estimated. Short term investments will often depend on the level of cash balances available for investment. The cash flow forecast will enable these levels to be estimated and hence help with the accuracy of the interest forecast.

Income and Expenditure Forecast

An example of a traditional format for an income and expenditure forecast is shown as follows:

A 20 place local authority nursing home is this year about to offer 25% of its places to fee paying private clients. It is also having to establish a trading account so that it's financial viability can be managed with a view to future competitive tendering. In order to assist with the process the home has produced an income and expenditure account based on the following assumptions.

- An annual grant is received for £600,000. This will be paid quarterly in advance

- Fees of £1000 per month are charged for each private place. It is assumed that only four out of the five places are filled for the year

- Fund-raising activities raise £12,000 for the year, from two main activities, one in the summer and one in the winter

- Employee Costs are £480,000, with no joiners or leavers during the year

- Operational Costs are estimated at £12,000 per month

- Support Service Costs are estimated at £2,000 per month

Income And Expenditure Forecast

	Apr	May	Jun	Jul	Aug	Sep	Oct	Nov	Dec	Jan	Feb	Mar	Total
Income (£'000)													
Grant	150			150			150			150			600
Fees	4	4	4	4	4	4	4	4	4	4	4	4	48
Fund-raising				6					6				12
Total	154	4	4	160	4	4	154	4	10	154	4	4	660
Expenditure (£,000)													
Employee Costs	40	40	40	40	40	40	40	40	40	40	40	40	480
Operational Costs	12	12	12	12	12	12	12	12	12	12	12	12	144
Support Service Costs	2	2	2	2	2	2	2	2	2	2	2	2	24
Total	54	54	54	54	54	54	54	54	54	54	54	54	648
Net Surplus/ Deficit	100	-50	-50	106	-50	-50	100	-50	-44	100	-50	-50	12

The above forecast can be developed either manually or by using a spreadsheet program. The forecast should be accompanied by detailed assumptions showing how the figures have been arrived at.

This forecast can then be monitored when undertaking financial control procedures. The total figures can be used as the annual budget, and the month by month forecasts can be referred to as a profiled budget.

Cash Flow Forecast

The cash flow forecast is developed using the income and expenditure forecast. The cash flow forecast reflects the timing of receipts and payments and shows the impact on the organisation's cash balances. The purpose of the cash flow forecast is to assist in financial control, which is discussed later in this chapter, and treasury management. It helps the organisation identify when cash shortages and cash surpluses are likely to arise such that the appropriate arrangements can be made.

The cash flow forecast looks similar in appearance to the income and expenditure forecast shown earlier, however the figures will not be the same. As with the income and expenditure forecast, the assumptions made need to be set out. These assumptions will include the estimated timing of receipts and payments. Most importantly any income not received before the end of the financial year will be referred to as debtors and expenditure payments not made before the end of the financial year will be referred to as creditors. Receipts from debtors and payments to creditors will be reflected in the following years cash flow. For example, if income due in March of £5,000 is not shown as a cash receipt in March, it will then be treated as a debtor at the end of the year. If it is likely that the cash will be received in April or May of the following year, it will be reflected in the following year's cash flow.

Given the income and expenditure example shown earlier a cash flow forecast can be developed based on the following assumptions:

- The grant is paid quarterly in advance
- Fees from private clients are paid monthly in arrears
- Money from fund-raising is all received in the month that it is earned
- Salaries are paid at the end of each month
- Operational costs are paid 2 months in arrears
- Support service costs are paid monthly at the beginning of each month

Cash Flow Forecast

	Apr	May	Jun	Jul	Aug	Sep	Oct	Nov	Dec	Jan	Feb	Mar	Total
Income (£'000)													
Grant	150			150			150			150			600
Fees		4	4	4	4	4	4	4	4	4	4	4	44
Fund-raising				6					6				12
Total	150	4	4	160	4	4	154	4	10	154	4	4	656
Expenditure (£,000)													
Employee Costs	40	40	40	40	40	40	40	40	40	40	40	40	480
Operational Costs			12	12	12	12	12	12	12	12	12	12	120
Support Service Costs	2	2	2	2	2	2	2	2	2	2	2	2	24
Total	42	42	54	54	54	54	54	54	54	54	54	54	624
Balance mth	108	-38	-50	106	-50	-50	100	-50	-44	100	-50	-50	32
Cash b/f	0	108	70	20	126	76	26	126	76	32	132	82	0
Cash c/f	108	70	20	126	76	26	126	76	32	132	82	32	32

It can be seen from the cash flow forecast that there will be positive cash balances each month if the assumptions prove to be accurate.

There will also be a debtor of £4,000 in respect of fees not yet received and a creditor of £24,000 in respect of operational costs not yet paid.

Financial Control Techniques

There are many financial control techniques that should be adopted throughout the year in order to ensure that an organisation is able to meet its financial targets in all respects. These include:

❖ Monitoring income and expenditure forecasts

❖ Monitoring cash flow forecasts

❖ Calculating variances and taking action to correct adverse variances

❖ Undertaking re-forecasts to reflect the impact of actual figures on the future

Some organisations may separate revenue and capital forecasts such that they can be monitored separately.

It is advisable that an organisation undertakes a re-forecast every month or every quarter. This is where the actual figures achieved for the month replace the estimates and new estimates are included into the future months in order to reflect current events, changes in assumptions, and corrective action. As a result of re-forecasting the organisation can project the likely financial outturn at the end of the year given what has currently taken place and the future corrective actions. This allows the organisation to predict its likely end of year financial performance, and assists with long term planning.

SUMMARY

☐ Financial planning involves looking ahead at all the financial requirements of the organisation, and identifying how they can be met over the time horizon being considered

☐ In order to control finances, there needs to be a plan to start with otherwise there is no benchmark against which to measure performance over the year. Control therefore has to be within a framework which is set by the financial plan

☐ Public sector organisations should set targets with respect to service delivery for the future. This should identify the type, quality and quantity of service to be provided

☐ All forecasts require assumptions to be made, and income forecasts require assumptions to be as prudent as possible because unlike expenditure which can be subject to a certain amount of internal control, income is often subject to external forces

☐ There are many financial control techniques that should be adopted throughout the year in order to ensure that an organisation is able to meet its financial targets in all respects

Exercise 12

Calculating an Income and Expenditure Forecast

A nursery school has 35 places which are subsidised by a grant of £48,000 per year. Fees are collected from parents on a weekly basis of £100 per week. The grant is expected quarterly in advance whereas fees are paid at the end of each week. Further income is derived from fundraising events such as raffles, fetes, sponsored walks, etc. These tend to net £200 per month. Donations are also obtained from local companies, and it is hoped that £1,200 will be raised during the year. Salaries tend to be static throughout the year at £13,000 per month. Catering costs are £1200 per month and uniforms of £2,000 are purchased in September and March each year. Toys and playthings average at £4,800 for the year and other supplies and services are approximately £1,000 per month. The rent of £20,000 is paid quarterly in advance and includes all accommodation costs. Other miscellaneous expenditure is £500 per month (this includes petty cash, staff expenses, etc.).

Using the proforma provided on pages 88 and 89, calculate the income and expenditure forecast based on the above information. (Assume 4 weeks in each month.)

Nursery School Income and Expenditure Forecast

	Apr	May	Jun	Jul	Aug	Sep
INCOME						
Grant						
Fees						
Fundraising						
Donation						
Total						
EXPENDITURE						
Salaries						
Catering						
Uniforms						
Toys						
Supplies & Services						
Rent						
Sundry						
Total						
Surplus/Deficit						

Oct	Nov	Dec	Jan	Feb	Mar	Total

Suggested solutions to this exercise can be found on page 134

Exercise 13

Calculating a Cash Flow Forecast

With respect to the nursery schools financial position outlined in exercise 12, the following further information is given.

- With the exception of catering, all suppliers are paid one month in arrears

- On average only 80% of parents fees are received on time with the other 20% being paid one month in arrears

- Half the donations appear to be received around Christmas and the other half in March

Complete the pro-forma cash flow forecast for the nursery

Nursery School Cash Flow Forecast

	Apr	May	Jun	Jul	Aug	Sep
RECEIPTS						
PAYMENTS						
TOTAL						
Bal. Month						
Bal. b/f						
Bal. c/f						

Oct	Nov	Dec	Jan	Feb	Mar	Total

Suggested solutions to this exercise can be found on page 135

Exercise 14

Re-forecasting

The nursery described in exercises 12 and 13 have had three months of actual operation and the actual cash flow figures are shown in the proforma cash flow forecast sheet overleaf. The fundraising committee have not organised any events to date, but intend to get back to monthly activity as from August. The quarterly grant payments seem to be coming a month later than they should do. All other payments are following the original cash flow projection pattern with the exception of supplies and services which have increased to an average of £1200 per month, and catering which has decreased by £200 per month.

The nursery requires a re-forecast cash flow taking into account the above changes and they wish to know how much their overdraft facility needs to be.

Use the proforma to undertake the re-forecast calculations.

Nursery School Cash Flow Re-forecast

	Apr	May	Jun	Jul	Aug	Sep
RECEIPTS						
Grant		12,000				
Fees	11,200	14,000	14,000			
Fundraising						
Donation						
Total	11,200	26,000	14,000			
PAYMENTS						
Salaries	13,000	13,000	13,000			
Catering	1,000	1,000	1,000			
Uniforms						
Toys		400	400			
Supplies & Services		1,200	1,200			
Rent	5,000					
Sundry	500	500	500			
TOTAL	19,500	16,100	16,100			
Bal. Month	-8,300	9,900	-2,100			
Bal. b/f	0	-8,300	1,600			
Bal. c/f	-8,300	1,600	-500			

Oct	Nov	Dec	Jan	Feb	Mar	Total

Overdraft facility should be £ ☐

Suggested solutions to this exercise can be found on page 136

Exercise 15

Your Own Financial Forecasts

If possible complete the pro-forma income and expenditure, and cash flow forecast with figures from your own organisation. If you do not have accurate figures estimates will do.

Income and Expenditure Forecast

	Apr	May	Jun	Jul	Aug	Sep
INCOME						
Total						
EXPENDITURE						
Total						
Surplus/Deficit						

Oct	Nov	Dec	Jan	Feb	Mar	Total

Cash Flow Forecast

	Apr	May	Jun	Jul	Aug	Sep
RECEIPTS						
PAYMENTS						
TOTAL						
Bal. Month						
Bal. b/f						
Bal. c/f						

Oct	Nov	Dec	Jan	Feb	Mar	Total

Chapter 8

KEY FINANCIAL TERMS

A

Account

A record of financial transactions.

Accounting Period

The period of time covered by the accounts of an organisation. Usually it refers to the financial year, which for most public sector organisations is 1 April to 31 March, however, an accounting period may cover any length of time.

Accounting system

The means by which transactions are recorded thus enabling the production of financial accounts.

Accrual

An accounting entry that reflects the usage of goods or services yet to be invoiced at the end of the accounting period. The accrual estimates the value of such use and sets up a credit item to reflect that the organisation "owes" the suppliers even though an official invoice has not yet been received. Most common accruals relate to items such as the telephone and utilities where bills are usually only raised quarterly.

Assets

What the organisation owns, such as property, equipment and cash.

Audit

An independent examination of an organisation's activities, either by internal audit or the organisation's external auditors.

Internal audit provides an independent function within an organisation, for the review of activities and as a service to all levels of management. It is a managerial control mechanism which measures and evaluates the effectiveness of financial and other controls.

External audit provides the independent examination of, and expression of opinion on, the annual financial statements of an organisation, as required by legislation.

Audit Report

A report provided by the external auditors stating their opinion of the financial statements. The report usually includes the term "true and fair view".

B

Bank Reconciliation

A statement explaining the difference between the balance of an account reported by a bank statement and the bank account appearing in the books of the organisation.

Bankruptcy

When an individual cannot, nor has the prospect of being able to meet debts as they become due. This is similar to insolvency for a corporate body. Bankruptcy has to be determined legally, in other words by the courts.

Base Rate

The interest rate which financial institutions use as a bench mark for determining the interest rate they expect potential borrowers to pay. Most lending is undertaken at a number of percentage points above base rate, as in "2% over base".

Books of Account

A set of books which record the financial transactions of an organisation.

Budget

An estimate of income and expenditure planned by an organisation for a particular period of time, usually at least a year.

Business Plan

A document often used to assist in raising finance and in strategic planning. It is the result of the business planning process.

Business Planning Process

This is a process whereby an organisation performs a structured appraisal of its objectives, and analyses its current position with regard to its activities, resources and the environment in which it operates; and develops a set of strategic action plans in order to achieve its objectives, taking into account all the financial implications of those actions.

Bad Debt

Money owed by customers but written off in the accounts because it can not be collected.

Balance Sheet

A statement showing what the organisation owns and owes at any particular time. It lists the nature of the assets and liabilities of the organisation. In all cases, assets always equal liabilities.

C

Capital

The finance supplied to acquire the resources (assets) and to fund the day to day activities of the organisation with which to operate in the first instance. Fixed capital is invested in land, buildings, machinery, vehicles, etc.; working capital circulates within the organisation with respect to day to day transactions.

Capital Expenditure

Money spent on assets not used up during a year but which have a continuing value to the organisation e.g. buildings and equipment.

Cash Book

A book in which an account (record) is kept of all receipts and payments of money, by cash or cheque.

Cash Flow

Movement of money through the organisation, from buying materials, paying expenses, producing goods and services, selling the service and receiving payment.

Cash Flow Forecasts

An estimate of the future movement of money through the organisation, to help predict the cash requirements during the year.

Closing of the Books

The periodical closing off and adjusting of all accounts in the books of account, in order to report on income and expenditure during a period and the ensuing surplus or deficit and the level of assets and liabilities of the organisation.

Commitments

Expenditure in respect of goods, services and work for which orders have been placed or tenders accepted but for which payment has not been made.

Contingency

A sum set aside to provide for foreseen but unquantifiable future commitments or for unforeseen expenditure which may become necessary during the year.

Cost Centre

The term for each individual unit to which items of income and expenditure are charged for either managerial or detailed control purposes e.g. a vehicle, a school, a department.

Credit

Part of the double entry system (see debit).

Creditors (accounts payable)

These are the suppliers of goods and services to whom payment is due.

Current Liabilities

These include the amounts owing by the organisation which fall due for payment within one year.

Customs and Excise

A government department responsible for the administration and collection of Value Added Tax (VAT).

D

Debit

Part of the double entry accounting procedures, opposite to credit. A debit is made in relation to an increase in assets; a decrease in liabilities; an increase in expenses; or a decrease in income.

Debtors (accounts receivable)

These are the customers or organisations who owe money to the organisation for goods and services provided.

Double-entry

Method of book-keeping in which two entries are made in the books of account for each transaction reflecting the dual effect every transaction has on the organisation. For example, if a telephone bill is paid it increases the telephone expenditure and decreases the cash asset. These entries are often referred to as debit and credit entries.

E

Equity

The owners initial capital introduced to a business plus any retained surpluses/accumulated reserves.

Estimate

A method of informing a potential customer of the approximate price of your goods and services. It is a carefully worked out approximation, not a fixed price. This means you are entitled in law to change the price if necessary.

F

Fixed Assets

These are the assets with continuing value, typically land, premises, plant and machinery.

Financial Regulations

A written code agreed by an organisation to provide a framework in which to conduct its financial affairs.

Fixed Costs

These are the costs which do not vary with productivity such as rent.

Forecast

An expression of an organisation's long term plan in financial terms. The forecast predicts future income and expenditure. The two main forecasts used in planning are the Income and Expenditure Forecast and Cash Flow Forecast.

G

General Ledger

The principal book of account consolidating all the other books of account such as the cash book, purchase ledger, sales ledger, and so on.

Going Concern

An organisational status whereby the organisation is in a position to continue its operations into the foreseeable future, i.e. it is a going concern.

Goodwill

This represents the difference between the total paid for an acquired business and the value of the net assets taken over. Goodwill is an intangible asset and not necessarily capable of accurate measurement.

Gross

A total without any deductions.

Gross Margin

The difference between the selling price of goods and the unit cost of production, excluding overheads.

Gross Profit

Sales or turnover for a period less the cost of production, excluding overheads.

H

Historic Cost

Fixed Assets are normally shown at historic cost in the balance sheet; the cost at which they were originally purchased.

I

Income

Amounts due to an organisation which have been or are expected to be received. Public sector income includes rents, fees and charges, sales, grants and rates. The term 'income' implies that the figures concerned relate to amounts due in respect of an accounting period, irrespective of whether or not they have been received.

Inflation

This is the effect brought about by rising prices, which lower the value of money.

Inland Revenue

A government department which deals with the collection of taxes on various types of income, such as income tax.

Insolvent

When an organisation's assets are less than their liabilities and they are unable to meet their liabilities when they fall due.

Insurance

Protection against risk.

Intangible Assets

These are assets which have no physical existence, e.g. an asset which is neither fixed nor current, yet possesses a value, such as goodwill, copyright or intellectual property.

Internal Auditor

See "Audit" except this type of auditor is not independent of the organisation but audits departments within the organisation.

Invoice

A document showing the character, quantity, price, terms, nature of delivery and other particulars of goods sold or services rendered.

J

Journal Entry

A record of a transaction adjusting the main books of account, usually used for changes such as correcting errors or allocating expenditure between different cost centres.

L

Liability

An amount owed to an individual or organisation which will be paid at some time in the future. Liabilities include both money borrowed, but not yet repaid and payments due to creditors.

Liquid Assets

These include cash and easily realisable assets, such as debtors or short-term investments.

Liquidity
A measure of an organisation's ability to pay it's liabilities as they fall due.

Long Term Liabilities
Liabilities of an organisation, whose payment period is greater than one year.

M

Management Accounts
These are internal tailor-made financial statements and reports prepared as required, to assist the management of an organisation control its financial resources on a day to day basis, and to inform their decision making.

N

Net Assets
This represents total assets less liabilities. It is the amount usually described as Capital Employed, a component figure of the Return on Capital Employed (ROCE) ratio.

Net Book Value
Represents the value of fixed assets at a point in time. It is calculated as cost less accumulated depreciation.

Net Profit
The profit gained after deducting overheads from gross profit.

Net Worth

Also known as net assets, this figure is found by fixed assets plus net current assets or working capital (current assets - current liabilities) less long term liabilities.

Nominal Ledger

Otherwise known as the general ledger.

O

Overheads

Support costs as opposed to operational or direct costs. Sometimes these are not directly allocated to a cost centre but apportioned between cost centres by way of an agreed procedure.

P

Petty Cash

Money available for cash transactions, usually small in nature.

Petty Cash Book

A book subsidiary to the cash book in which all petty cash transactions are recorded.

Profit and Loss Account

A statement of all income and revenue expenditure, showing, as its balance, the profit or loss for the accounting period. This can be referred to as an income and expenditure account with its balance being a surplus or deficit.

Provisions

Amounts set aside for specific liabilities of which the organisation is aware at the time of the preparation of the accounts, e.g. provision for depreciation and bad debts. Provisions are added to expenditure and therefore have the impact of reducing surpluses.

Q

Qualified Audit Report

An audit report which contains words "subject to" or "except for".

R

Receivers

An accountant appointed by a secured creditor in order to secure as much of the debt, owed to that creditor, as possible. Receivers will normally try to continue the business aiming to sell it as a going concern.

Recharge

An internal transaction whereby one cost centre recharges another cost centre for services provided.

Revenue Expenditure

The day to day expenses an organisation incurs in providing its services (as opposed to capital expenditure).

S

Sensitivity Analysis

Method of examining the performance of cash flow and other forecasting models when variables and/or assumptions are altered.

Solvent

A situation where an organisation is able to meet all of its short and long term liabilities.

Standing Orders

Formal rules an organisation draws up to regulate its proceedings and the conduct of its activities. Standing orders will cover all key areas such as finance.

Suspense Account

An account which is used for receipts or payment that cannot immediately be correctly allocated to a specific account. This is usually because of inadequate information.

T

Tangible Assets

These are assets with a physical existence such as land, premises, plant, equipment etc.

U

Undercutting

Selling below the prices of competitors.

V

Variable Costs
Costs which vary with productivity, i.e. in accordance with the volume or level of service provided.

Variance
The differences between actual and budgeted figures.

Viability
A project is viable if it can be undertaken without loss to those responsible for it.

Virement
The transfer of an underspending on one budget head to finance additional spending on another budget head, in accordance with an organisation's financial regulations, and standing orders.

W

Working Capital
The sums available to meet the day to day expense of maintaining an operation. Working capital is usually calculated as current assets less current liabilities.

Write Off
Charging an item as an expense against surplus in a particular period.

Z

Zero Growth

No additional expenditure over that spent in a previous year.

Solutions to Exercises

SOLUTIONS TO EXERCISES

Solution to Exercise 13

Solution to Exercise 14

Solution to Exercise 1
Accounting Entries

a) A fire officer purchases new uniforms for £10,000 but has yet to pay the supplier.

Increase in expenditure account on uniforms	£10,000
Increase in creditors (people we owe money to)	£10,000

b) A doctor charges £50 for writing a letter on behalf of a client for which the client had to pay in advance.

Increase in fees	£50
Increase in cash	£50

c) A school contracts out its cleaning services to a private contractor and has to pay £24,000 a year in monthly instalments. Show the entries for this month.

Increase in expenditure on cleaning contract	£2,000
Decrease in cash	£2,000

d)   The planning department advised three clients during the week all of whom were charged £200 each for advice. Two paid immediately, however, the third has yet to pay.

Increase in fees	£600
Increase in cash	£400
Increase in debtors (people who owe us money)	£200

e)   Three managers of the local authority grounds maintenance service decide to set up their own company in order to bid independently for contracts. To start it off, they all invest £10,000 each in the new company.

Increase in cash	£30,000
Increase in Owners Equity (could use the term capital or investment)	£30,000

Solution to Exercise 3
Which Financial Statement?

	Income and Expenditure	Balance Sheet
Cash in bank		X
Fees	X	
Motor vehicles		X
Creditors		X
Stationery	X	
Rent	X	
Grants	X	
Overdraft		X
Computer maintenance	X	
Depreciation	X	
Debtors		X
Office furniture		X
Insurance	X	
Loan		X
Bank interest	X	
Salaries	X	
Reserves		X

Solution to Exercise 4
Preparing a Trading Account

	£	£
Income:		
Fees		180,000
Expenditure:		
Direct costs	45,000	
Consultant fees	20,000	
Salaries	38,000	
Office overheads	6,000	
Other charges	5,000	
Loan interest	5,000	
Depreciation	15,000	
Total		134,000
Surplus or Deficit for the year		46,000

Solution to Exercise 5
Preparing an Income and Expenditure Account

Limit H.A.
Income and Expenditure Account
for the year ended 19XX

INCOME

Trading and Operations	1,950,000	
Other income (interest)	15,000	
		1,965,000

EXPENDITURE

Direct Expenditure	1,885,000	
Central Costs	45,000	
Interest Payments	65,000	
Depreciation	10,000	
		2,005,000

Deficit for the Year	**(40,000)**

Solution to Exercise 8
Calculating the Balance Sheet

	Cost £	Depreciation £	NBV £	
Fixed Assets				
Equipment	100,000	15,000	85,000	A
Current Assets				
Debtors	72,000			
Cash	0			
(sub total x)		72,000		
Current Liabilities				
Creditors	0			
Overdraft	11,000			
(sub total y)		11,000		
Net Current Assets (x-y)			61,000	B
Net Assets			146,000	A+B
Represented by				
Surplus for the year from the trading account		46,000		
Loan		100,000		
(A+B) should equal C			146,000	C

Calculation Notes:

1. Calculate the cash balance for the year as follows:

    Cash Received (£180,000-40% outstanding £72,000)   £108,000
    Cash paid (all the expenditure less the depreciation)   £119,000
    Overdraft   **-£11,000**

2. Calculate the debtors 40% of £180,000   **£72,000**

3. Calculate the depreciation 15% of £100,000   **£15,000**
    and subtract from the cost of the
    equipment to give a net book value (NBV)   **£85,000**

4. Surplus was calculated from exercise 4   **£46,000**

Solution to Exercise 9
Calculating Key Financial Ratios

	Year 1	Year 2
a) R.O.C.E.	$\dfrac{16,000}{100,000}$ = 16%	$\dfrac{17,000}{100,000}$ = 17%
Surplus Percentage	$\dfrac{16,000}{600,000}$ = 2.67%	$\dfrac{17,000}{700,000}$ = 2.43%
Income Growth		$\dfrac{700,000-600,000}{600,000}$ = 16.67%

b) Additional information needed should include:

- Budget Information - planned income and expenditure
- Performance Targets - planned rates of return
- Business Plan - planned service output
- Balance Sheet - liquidity levels, especially level of debtors

Solution to Exercise 10
Interpretation of Financial Ratios

An argument could be made for both health centres to remain open, particularly as they are both making a surplus. However, if one does have to close then based on the information given at face value it should be Health Centre 1, for the following reasons:

- It has a higher capital base (£50,000[1] compared with £24,000[2])and hence releases more capital on closure.

$$(1) \quad \frac{5,000}{10\%} \qquad\qquad (2) \quad \frac{600}{2.5\%}$$

- There is a low liquidity level, and even more worrying is the high level of debtors, and slow debt collection rates compared to the other health centre (110, compared with 73 days)

- Even though both health centres have a negative variance on their budgeted surplus, health centre 1 has a significantly higher one, especially given that the increase in productivity is only half a percent compared with the 6 percent of health centre 2.

What is clear is that a number of other factors would affect the decision such as:

- **Location of the centres**
  Impact on cost, impact on number of users, etc.

- **Number of users**
  Impact on cost

- **Physical condition**
  Potential need for refurbishment could lead to greater cost

- **Maximum capacity**
  Impact on the potential for expansion to cope with effect of closure of the other health centre

Solution to Exercise 11
Understanding Your Cash Flow

Question	score		Question	score		Question	score
1 a	2		**2** a	4		**3** a	1
b	1		b	2		b	4
c	4						
d	3						
4 a	4		**5** a	1		**6** a	1
b	2		b	2		b	3
c	3		c	4		c	4
7 a	4		**8** a	3		**9** a	1
b	2		b	1		b	3
10 a	4						
b	2						
c	1						

Over 25

Cash seems to be very tight within the organisation, and even slight delays in the timing of cash receipts could cause a cash crisis. The organisation should always make sure that a cash flow forecast is produced and updated regularly such that the extent of any overdraft requirements are known well in advance. If possible, the organisation should arrange overdraft facilities that are in excess of their needs to prevent the chances of shortages in cash. The organisation should also examine its sources of funds and try to maximise the speed of cash collection using effective credit control procedures.

16 to 25

Cash flow seems to be stable and does not present a problem at the moment. However, the organisation is not sufficiently robust to ignore the timing of cash receipts and payments. There is a need for close monitoring of balances to ensure that the cash position always remains in control.

15 or less

The organisation does not have any problems with cash levels and appears to be in a very strong position with regard to cash flows. The organisation has to concentrate its efforts on treasury management and ensuring that it maximises the income earned by any cash surpluses.

Solution to Exercise 12
Calculating an Income and Expenditure Forecast

Nursery School Income and Expenditure Forecast

	Apr	May	Jun	Jul	Aug	Sep	Oct	Nov	Dec	Jan	Feb	Mar	Total
INCOME													
Grant	12,000			12,000			12,000			12,000			48,000
Fees	14,000	14,000	14,000	14,000	14,000	14,000	14,000	14,000	14,000	14,000	14,000	14,000	168,000
Fundraising	200	200	200	200	200	200	200	200	200	200	200	200	2,400
Donation	100	100	100	100	100	100	100	100	100	100	100	100	1,200
TOTAL	26,300	14,300	14,300	26,300	14,300	14,300	26,300	14,300	14,300	26,300	14,300	14,300	219,600
EXPENDITURE													
Salaries	13,000	13,000	13,000	13,000	13,000	13,000	13,000	13,000	13,000	13,000	13,000	13,000	156,000
Catering	1,200	1,200	1,200	1,200	1,200	1,200	1,200	1,200	1,200	1,200	1,200	1,200	14,400
Uniforms						2,000						2,000	4,000
Toys	400	400	400	400	400	400	400	400	400	400	400	400	4,800
Supplies & Services	1,000	1,000	1,000	1,000	1,000	1,000	1,000	1,000	1,000	1,000	1,000	1,000	12,000
Rent	5,000			5,000			5,000			5,000			20,000
Sundry	500	500	500	500	500	500	500	500	500	500	500	500	6,000
TOTAL	21,100	16,100	16,100	21,100	16,100	18,100	21,100	16,100	16,100	21,100	16,100	18,100	217,200
Surplus/Deficit	5,200	-1,800	-1,800	5,200	-1,800	-3,800	5,200	-1,800	-1,800	5,200	-1,800	-3,800	2,400

Solution to Exercise 13
Calculating a Cash Flow Forecast

Nursery School Cash Flow Forecast

	Apr	May	Jun	Jul	Aug	Sep	Oct	Nov	Dec	Jan	Feb	Mar	Total
Receipts													
Grant	12,000			12,000			12,000			12,000			48,000
Fees	11,200	14,000	14,000	14,000	14,000	14,000	14,000	14,000	14,000	14,000	14,000	14,000	165,200
Fundraising	200	200	200	200	200	200	200	200	200	200	200	200	2,400
Donation									600			600	1,200
TOTAL	23,400	14,200	14,200	26,200	14,200	14,200	26,200	14,200	14,800	26,200	14,200	14,800	216,800
Payments													
Salaries	13,000	13,000	13,000	13,000	13,000	13,000	13,000	13,000	13,000	13,000	13,000	13,000	156,000
Catering	1,200	1,200	1,200	1,200	1,200	1,200	1,200	1,200	1,200	1,200	1,200	1,200	14,400
Uniforms							2,000						2,000
Toys		400	400	400	400	400	400	400	400	400	400	400	4,400
Supplies & Services		1,000	1,000	1,000	1,000	1,000	1,000	1,000	1,000	1,000	1,000	1,000	11,000
Rent	5,000			5,000			5,000			5,000			20,000
Sundry	500	500	500	500	500	500	500	500	500	500	500	500	6,000
TOTAL	19,700	16,100	16,100	21,100	16,100	16,100	23,100	16,100	16,100	21,100	16,100	16,100	213,800
Bal Month	3,700	-1,900	-1,900	5,100	-1,900	-1,900	3,100	-1,900	-1,300	5,100	-1,900	-1,300	3,000
Bal b/f	0	3,700	1,800	-100	5,000	3,100	1,200	4,300	2,400	1,100	6,200	4,300	0
Bal c/f	3,700	1,800	-100	5,000	3,100	1,200	4,300	2,400	1,100	6,200	4,300	3,000	3,000

Solution to Exercise 14
Re-Forecasting

Nursery School Cash Flow Re-forecast

	Apr	May	Jun	Jul	Aug	Sep	Oct	Nov	Dec	Jan	Feb	Mar	Total
Receipts													
Grant		12,000			12,000			12,000			12,000		48,000
Fees	11,200	14,000	14,000	14,000	14,000	14,000	14,000	14,000	14,000	14,000	14,000	14,000	165,200
Fundraising					200	200	200	200	200	200	200	200	1,600
Donation									600			600	1,200
TOTAL	11,200	26,000	14,000	14,000	26,200	14,200	14,200	26,200	14,800	14,200	26,200	14,800	216,000
Payments													
Salaries	13,000	13,000	13,000	13,000	13,000	13,000	13,000	13,000	13,000	13,000	13,000	13,000	156,000
Catering	1,000	1,000	1,000	1,000	1,000	1,000	1,000	1,000	1,000	1,000	1,000	1,000	12,000
Uniforms							2,000						2,000
Toys		400	400	400	400	400	400	400	400	400	400	400	4,400
Supplies & Services		1,200	1,200	1,200	1,200	1,200	1,200	1,200	1,200	1,200	1,200	1,200	13,200
Rent	5,000			5,000			5,000			5,000			20,000
Sundry	500	500	500	500	500	500	500	500	500	500	500	500	6,000
TOTAL	19,500	16,100	16,100	21,100	16,100	16,100	23,100	16,100	16,100	21,100	16,100	16,100	213,600
Bal Month	-8,300	9,900	-2,100	-7,100	10,100	-1,900	-8,900	10,100	-1,300	-6,900	10,100	-1,300	2,400
Bal b/f	0	-8,300	1,600	-500	-7,600	2,500	600	-8,300	1,800	500	-6,400	3,700	0
Bal c/f	-8,300	1,600	-500	-7,600	2,500	600	-8,300	1,800	500	-6,400	3,700	2,400	2,400

Overdraft facilities would be in excess of £8,300

Index

Index

A

Account   103
Accountability   1
Accounting Period   103
Accounting System   103
Accruals   21, 22, 103
Acid Test   56
Asset Rent   55
Assets   3, 37, 43, 45, 104
  Current   41, 52
  Fixed   38, 52, 109
  Intangible   40, 112
  Net   52, 113
  Tangible   116
Assumptions   86
Audit   104

B

Bad Debts   23, 106
Balance Sheet   6, 8, 37, 40, 44, 45, 106
Bankruptcy   105
Base Rate   105
Book Keeping   4
Break-even   49
Budgets   50, 105
Business Plan   75, 105

C

Capital Assets   40
Capital Expenditure   20, 106
Capital Fund   43
Cash   41, 63
Cash Accounting   21

G

I

J

L

M